SCIENCE FAIR PROJECTS

Cells and Systems

Kelly Milner Halls

Heinemann Library
Chicago, Illinois

J 612
Halls

Customer Service 888-454-2279
Visit our website at www.heinemannlibrary.com

Designed by Kimberly R. Miracle and Fiona MacColl
Illustrations by Cavedweller Studios
Printed in China by WKT Ltd

11 10 09 08 07
10 9 8 7 6 5 4 3 2 1

ISBNs: ISBN-13: 978-1-4034-7909-9(hc)   ISBN-10: 1-4034-7909-7(hc)

Library of Congress Cataloging-in-Publication Data
Halls, Kelly Milner, 1957-
  Cells and systems / Kelly Milner Halls.
     p. cm. -- (Science fair projects)
  Includes index.
  ISBN-13: 978-1-4034-7909-9 (hc)
  1. Physiology--Experiments--Juvenile literature.. 2. Science projects--Juvenile literature. I. Title.
  QP42.H26 2007
  612--dc22
                              2006025459

Acknowledgments
The author and publishers are grateful to the following for permission to reproduce copyright
material: Alamy, **pp. 16** (Phototake Inc), **24** (DK); Corbis/zefa/Thorsten Rother, **p. 32**; Getty Images,
pp. 8 (Stone), **12**, **40** (3D4Medical.com); **26** (dk); **28** (Photonica); Masterfile/ Andrew Douglas, **p.
4**; Mediscan/Greenhill, **p. 36**; Science Photo Library, **p. 10** (Sinclair Stammers), **p. 34** (John Bavosi);
Wellcome/Medical Art Service, Munich, **p. 20**; Wellcome/Miles Kelly Art Library, **p.6**.

Cover photograph reproduced with permission of Getty Images/Visual Unlimited. Background
image by istockphoto.com.

Every effort has been made to contact copyright holders of any material reproduced
in this book. Any omissions will be rectified in subsequent printings if notice is given
to the publisher.

» Some words are shown in bold, **like this**. You can
find the definitions for these words in the glossary.

Contents

Science Fair Basics

Starting a science fair project can be an exciting challenge. You can test **scientific theory** by developing an appropriate scientific question. Then you can search, using the thoughtful steps of a well-planned experiment, for the answer to that question. It's like a treasure hunt of the mind.

In a way, your mission is to better understand how your world and the things in it work. You may be rewarded with a good grade or an award for your scientific hard work. But no matter what scores your project receives, you'll be a winner. That's because you will know a little bit more about your subject than you did before you started.

In this book, we'll look at nine different science fair projects related to cells and the way living bodies function. We will explore amazing mysteries hidden inside the human body.

Do Your Research

Is there something about the human body you've always wondered about? Something you don't quite understand but would like to? Then do a little research about the subject. Go to the library and check out books about the subject that interests you.

Use your favorite Internet search engine to find reliable online sources. Museums, universities, scientific journals, newspapers, and magazines are among the best sources for accurate research. Each experiment in this book lists some suggestions for further research.

When doing research you need to make sure your sources are reliable. Ask yourself the following questions about sources, especially those you find online.

The Experiments

The beginning of each experiment contains a box like this

Possible Question:

This question is a suggested starting point for your experiment. You will need to adapt the question to reflect your own interests.

Possible Hypothesis:

Don't worry if your hypothesis doesn't match the one listed here, this is only a suggestion.

Approximate Cost of Materials:

Discuss this with your parents before beginning work.

Materials Needed:

Make sure you can easily get all of the materials listed and gather them before beginning work.

Level of Difficulty:

There are three levels of experiments in this book: Easy, Intermediate, and Hard. The level of difficulty is based on how long the experiment takes and how complicated it is.

1) How old is the source? Is it possible that the information is outdated?

2) Who wrote the source? Is there an identifiable author, and is the author qualified to write about the topic?

3) What is the purpose of the source? The website of a potato chip company is probably not the best place to look for information on healthful diets.

4) Is the information well documented? Can you tell where the author got his or her information?

Some websites allow you to "chat" online with experts. Make sure you discuss this with your parent or teacher before participating. Never give out private information, including your address, online.

Once you know a little more about the subject you want to explore, you'll be ready to ask a science project question and form an intelligent **hypothesis**. A hypothesis is an educated guess about what the results of your experiment will be. Finally, you'll be ready to begin your science fair exploration!

What Is an Experiment?

When you say you're going to "experiment" you may just mean that you're going to try something out. When a scientist uses that word though, he or she means something else. In a proper experiment you have **variables** and a **control**. A variable is something that changes. The independent variable is the thing you purposely change as part of the experiment. The dependent variable is the change that happens in response to the thing you do. The controlled variables, or control group, are the things you do not change so that you have something to compare your outcomes to. Here's an example: Ten people have headaches. You give 5 people (Group A) asprins. You do not allow 5 people (Group B) to do anything for their headaches. Group A is the independent variable. The effects of the asprins are the dependent variable. Group B is a control group. To make sure the experiment is accurate though, you need to do it several times.

Some of the projects in this book are not proper experiments. They are projects designed to help you learn about a subject. You need to check with your teacher about whether these projects are appropriate for your science fair. Make sure you know all the science fair rules about what kinds of projects and materials are allowed before beginning.

Your Hypothesis

Once you've decided what question you're going to try to answer, you'll want to make a scientific **prediction** of what you'll discover through your science project. For example, if you wonder why your parents tell you to eat breakfast, your question might be "Does eating breakfast affect the way I behave?"

Remember, a hypothesis is an educated guess about how your experiment will turn out—what results you'll observe. So your hypothesis in response to the above question might be, "Eating breakfast helps me concentrate." The hypothesis is your best guess of how things might turn out when the experiment has been completed. It's also a good way to find out if you can actually complete the steps needed to answer your project question. If your question is, "Am I smart?," it will be impossible to prove your hypothesis, no matter what you make it. So, be sure the evidence to prove or disprove your hypothesis is actually within reach.

Research Journal

It is very important to keep careful notes about your project. From start to finish, make entries in your research journal so you won't have to rely on memory when it comes time to create your display. What time did you start your experiment? How long did you work on it each day? What were the **variables**, or things that changed, about your experimental setting? How did they change and why? What things did you overlook in planning your project? How did you solve the problems, once you discovered them?

These are the kinds of questions you'll answer in your research journal. No detail is too small when it comes to scientific research. You'll find some tips on writing your report and preparing a great display at the back of this book on pages 44–46. Use these and the tips in each project as guides, but don't be afraid to get creative. Make your display, and your project, your own.

Grow Baby Grow

Humans and cows have very similar **gestation** lengths. But how does their development differ? Are they as much alike as they are different? This project will explore those questions by comparing the developmental stages of humans and cows.

Do Your Research

This project deals with the earliest stages of development of humans and cows. It compares their rates of growth at those stages. Before you begin your project, do some research to find out more about the stages of human development, as well as the development of other mammals. Once you've done some research, you can tackle this project. Or, you may come up with your own unique project after you've read and learned more about the topic.

Here are some books and websites you could start with in your research:

» Parker, Steve. *Reproduction*. Chicago: Raintree, 2004.
» Nova Online: Life's Greatest Miracle: www.pbs.org/wgbh/nova/miracle/
» Dairy Cows: www.agr.state.nc.us/cyber/kidswrld/general/barnyard/ dairybn.htm

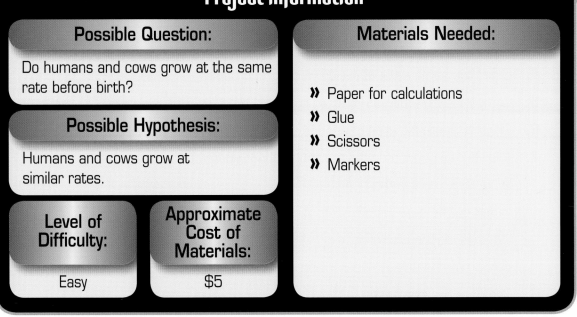

Project Information

Possible Question:

Do humans and cows grow at the same rate before birth?

Possible Hypothesis:

Humans and cows grow at similar rates.

Level of Difficulty:

Easy

Approximate Cost of Materials:

$5

Materials Needed:

» Paper for calculations
» Glue
» Scissors
» Markers

Steps to Success:

1. **NOTE:** This is a research project only, you will not be conducting an experiment. You should check with your teacher to make sure that this is appropriate for your science fair.

2. Research the growth of human and cow embryos.

3. Chart the stages and gestation period of a human embryo on graph paper.

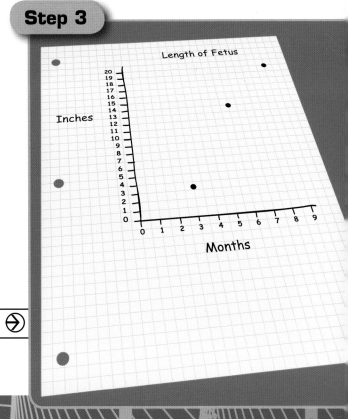

Step 3

Continued ➔

4. Chart the same **data** about cows on graph paper.

5. Compare both embryos at 2, 4, 6, and 8 months.

6. Draw or paste pictures of each of those four phases side by side.

7. Answer key developmental questions about each embryo:

   When can you see the heartbeat?

   When do the eyes form?

   When is motion visible?

   When can the embryo hear inside the **womb**?

8. Compare the responses to those questions.

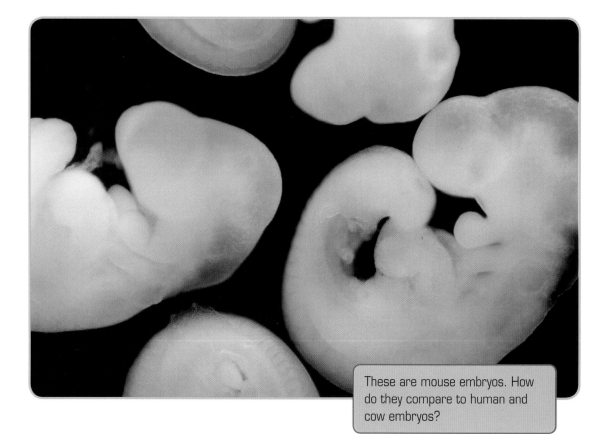

These are mouse embryos. How do they compare to human and cow embryos?

Result Summary:

» Did the human and cow embryos have similar growth phases?

Added Activities to Give Your Project Extra Punch:

» Interview a veterinarian, farmer, or other expert in cows about cow pregnancy and calf development. For assistance in finding an expert, contact the National 4H Council:
7100 Connecticut Avenue
Chevy Chase, Maryland 20815
(301) 961- 2800

» Compare the human embryo to an embryo of a non-mammal, such as a chicken.

» Compare the human embryo or cow embryo to that of a much larger or smaller mammal.

» Which animals take the longest to develop, and which take the least time? Why might that be?

» Compare the growth rates of various animals once they have been born. Why do different animals develop at different rates? How does this help or hurt them?

Display Extras:

» A slide projector or computer to show color images of the embryonic stages of both cows and humans.

» A series of embryonic pictures of other animals at the same stage of gestation.

The Building Blocks of Digestion

The human digestive system is an amazing thing. Under typical conditions, the stomach produces just enough **acid** to break down our food without breaking down our internal organs. But what does this process look like, and how long does it take for different foods to break down in the stomach? This experiment using vinegar to mimic stomach acid will help you find out.

Do Your Research

This project deals with how food is broken down in the stomach and how long that process takes for different kinds of food. Before you begin your project, do some research to find out more about the human stomach and digestive system, and how diet might affect health. Once you've done some research, you can tackle this project. Or, you may come up with your own unique project after you've read and learned more about the topic.

Here are some books and websites you could start with in your research:

» Ballard, Carol. *The Digestive System*. Chicago: Heinemann, 2003.
» Parker, Steve. *Digestion*. Chicago: Raintree, 2004.
» The Digestive System: www.imcpl.org/kids/guides/health/digestivesystem.html
» Discovery kids: www.yucky.kids.discovery.com/noflash/body/yuckystuff/gurgle/js.index.html

Project Information

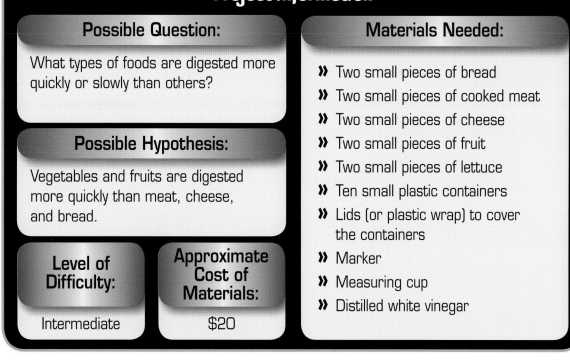

Possible Question:

What types of foods are digested more quickly or slowly than others?

Possible Hypothesis:

Vegetables and fruits are digested more quickly than meat, cheese, and bread.

Level of Difficulty:

Intermediate

Approximate Cost of Materials:

$20

Materials Needed:

» Two small pieces of bread
» Two small pieces of cooked meat
» Two small pieces of cheese
» Two small pieces of fruit
» Two small pieces of lettuce
» Ten small plastic containers
» Lids (or plastic wrap) to cover the containers
» Marker
» Measuring cup
» Distilled white vinegar

Steps to Success:

1. Pour 1/8 of a cup of vinegar in five of the plastic containers and mark them with a "V" so you'll remember later which ones contain vinegar.

2. Pour 1/8 of a cup of water in the other five plastic containers.

3. Put one piece of each of the five foods in the containers with vinegar.

4. Put the other pieces of the five foods, one each, in the containers with water.

Step 1

Continued ⊕

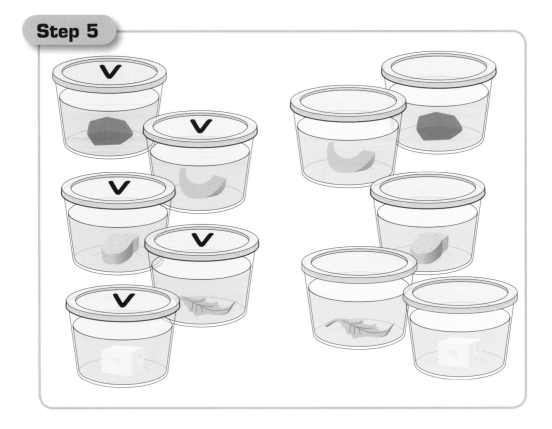

5. Cover the containers with lids or plastic wrap to hold the liquids (vinegar and water) in the dishes.

6. Check the food pieces every hour for six hours and record your observations.

7. Pay special attention to which foods broke down more easily than others, and whether or not acid or water made any difference.

NOTE: Make sure to discuss the proper disposal of food with a responsible adult.

Result Summary:

» Which foods seem to break down more quickly in the acid (vinegar)?

» Which foods seemed to resist breaking down in the vinegar?

» Did foods break down more quickly in the vinegar or water?

» How similar do you think the vinegar is to stomach acid?

Added Activities to Give Your Project Extra Punch:

» Repeat the steps using a highly processed "junk food" such as a candy bar or potato chips.

» Test the acidic liquid (vinegar) on other objects like chewing gum, pennies, and plastic or paper, and record and graph the results. (Be sure to check the ingredients of gum to help you predict what might happen with it.)

» Keep the foods in the containers until they are thoroughly broken down, checking them twice a day and recording how many days it takes for them to break down completely.

Display Extras:

» Photos of your foods every hour to show the process in action.

» Repeat the experiment as part of your project so the judges can examine for themselves. Include samples prepared in advance, a bit early, so people can observe the progress at one hour, three hours, and six hours during the short duration of the fair judging period. Make sure to check the science fair rules first.

» Photographs of partially digested foods.

Clearing the Air

Everyone knows smoking is bad for your health and the environment. If you've ever been curious about what smoke actually does to your lungs, this project will help show you what smoke is leaving behind.

Do Your Research

This project helps to demonstrate the effects that smoke from burning objects such as cigarettes has on absorbent objects like lungs. Before you begin your project, do some research to find out more about the effects of inhaling various kinds of smoke, the chemicals common in cigarettes, and the medical evidence of the damage smoke can do to the human body. Once you've done some research, you can tackle this project. Or, you may come up with your own unique project after you've read and learned more about the topic.

Here are some books and websites you could start with in your research:

» Bingham, Jane. *Smoking. What's the Deal?* Chicago: Heinemann, 2006.
» Parker, Steve. *Our Bodies: the Heart, Lungs, and Blood.* Chicago: Raintree, 2004.
» No Butts: What's in cigarettes?: http://nobutts.tamu.edu/facts/ingredients.htm
» American Lung Association:
   http://www.lungusa.org/site/pp.asp?c=dvLUK9OOE&b=22542
» Campaign for Tobacco Free Kids: http://tobaccofreekids.org

Project Information

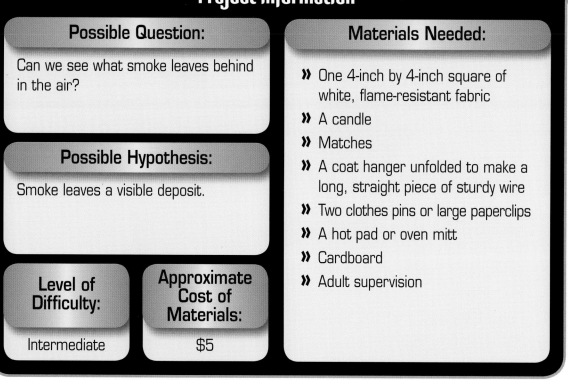

Possible Question:

Can we see what smoke leaves behind in the air?

Possible Hypothesis:

Smoke leaves a visible deposit.

Level of Difficulty:

Intermediate

Approximate Cost of Materials:

$5

Materials Needed:

» One 4-inch by 4-inch square of white, flame-resistant fabric
» A candle
» Matches
» A coat hanger unfolded to make a long, straight piece of sturdy wire
» Two clothes pins or large paperclips
» A hot pad or oven mitt
» Cardboard
» Adult supervision

Steps to Success:

1. Attach a piece of your cloth, partly folded, to the end of your hanger, using one pin or clip to attach two corners, and another to attach two more corners.

Step 1

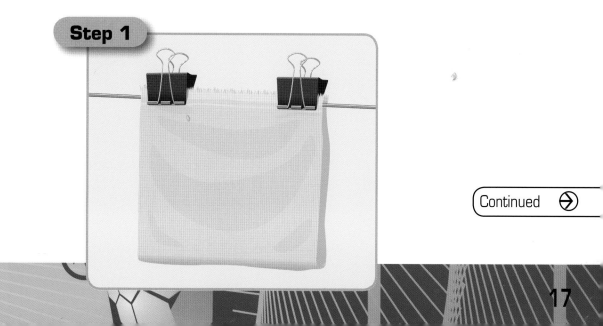

Continued ⟶

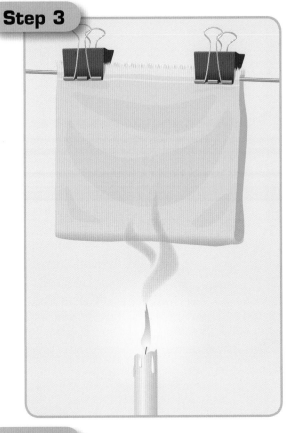

Step 3

ADULT
SUPERVISION
REQUIRED

2. Light the candle.

3. Using the hot pad or oven mitt in case the hanger gets got, hold the fold of the cloth six inches from the flame for five minutes. Make sure the smoke is flowing up to the fold in the cloth.

4. Remove the cloth from the flame and let the clothes hanger cool.

5. Carefully remove the cloth and staple it flat, fold side up, to cardboard to protect the visible results.

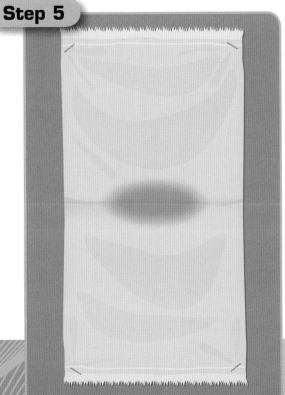

Step 5

Result Summary:

» How dirty did the smoke make your cloth sample?

» How could this compare to breathing in smoke, with it filtering through our lungs instead of cloth?

» Are all pollutants dangerous to our lungs?

Added Activities to Give Your Project Extra Punch:

» Repeat the test using a thin slice of raw meat instead of cloth. Raw meat is more similar to our lungs than cloth. Be sure to wash your hands carefully when working with raw meat.

» Repeat the test with a piece of bread to simulate the porous nature of lung tissue.

» If you live in an area where it can be safely done, and you have proper supervision, repeat the test creating a larger outdoor fire.

Display Extras:

» Be sure to display your final pieces of cloth and data.

» Display photographs of smokers' lungs vs. healthy lungs.

Be Still My Heart (But Not Too Still)

The human heart is a muscle that drives everything we do. It beats on, whether we sleep or run a dozen laps around the track. We know that the heartbeat changes depending on whether we're active or still. However, is the average **resting** and **active heart rate** the same for boys and girls? This experiment will help you find out.

Do Your Research

This project deals with the human heart and the effects that rest, activity, and gender have on the heartbeat. Before you begin your project, do some research to find out more about the human heart, its role in the functions of the human body, and how to accurately take a pulse. Once you've done some research, you can tackle this project. Or, you may come up with your own unique project after you've read and learned more about the topic.

Here are some books and websites you could start with in your research:

» Ballard, Carol. *Body Systems: Heart and Blood*. Chicago: Heinemann, 2003.

» Parker, Steve. *The Heart, Lungs, and Blood*. Chicago: Raintree, 2004.

» American Heart Association: http://www.americanheart.org

» The Heart: An Online Exploration: http://sln.fi.edu/biosci

Project Information

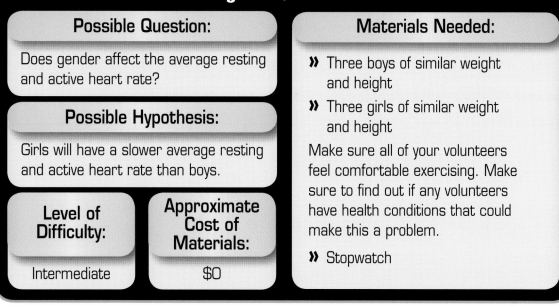

Possible Question:

Does gender affect the average resting and active heart rate?

Possible Hypothesis:

Girls will have a slower average resting and active heart rate than boys.

Level of Difficulty:

Intermediate

Approximate Cost of Materials:

$0

Materials Needed:

» Three boys of similar weight and height

» Three girls of similar weight and height

Make sure all of your volunteers feel comfortable exercising. Make sure to find out if any volunteers have health conditions that could make this a problem.

» Stopwatch

Steps to Success:

1. Have your volunteers sit quietly for at least half an hour. They could read a book or a magazine for 30 minutes before you follow step 2.

2. After your volunteers have rested for 30 minutes, check their pulses one at a time. Record the number of heartbeats you can count in 30 seconds in your research journal for each volunteer, noting whether they are girls or boys. Make sure your volunteers are quiet and resting while you do this.

3. Now, ask one of your volunteers to do 25 jumping jacks at a quick pace. It shouldn't take more than 30 seconds for the volunteer to do 25 jumping jacks.

4. Immediately after the last jumping jack, take the volunteer's pulse rate again. Record the number of heartbeats you count in 30 seconds in your research journal, and note whether the volunteer is a boy or girl.

Continued ➔

5. Repeat steps 3 and 4 with each volunteer until they have all completed the task, and record the results for each of them.

6. Add the girls' resting heart rates (before jumping jacks) together and divide by three to find the average resting heart rate for the girls. Do the same thing with their active heart rates (after jumping jacks) to find that average.

7. Follow the same process detailed in step 6 to find the average resting and active heart rates for the boys.

8. Compare the two sets of data to draw conclusions as to whether or not gender affects heart rate.

Step 2

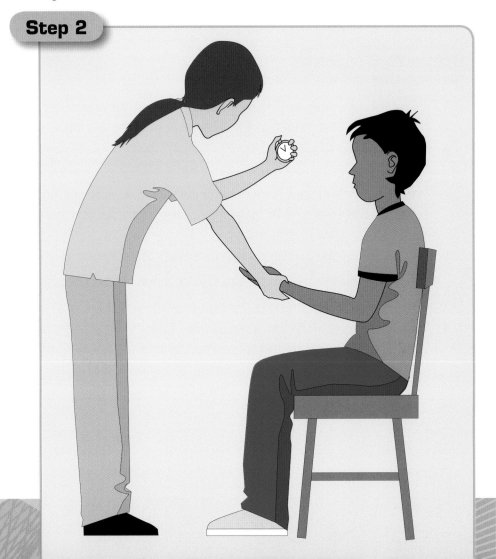

Result Summary:

» Did boys have a faster or slower resting heart rate than girls?

» Did girls have a faster or slower active heart rate than boys?

» Can you think of anything other than gender that might cause any differences you've observed?

Added Activities to Give Your Project Extra Punch:

» Compare boys' and girls' heart rates after researching their lifestyles — what hobbies do they have, and could those hobbies affect their heart rates?

» See if your results change when you use older volunteers like parents or teachers.

» Try using a larger sample (nine boys and nine girls) and see if you come up with the same results.

Display Extras:

» A heart model you can get from a hobby store and put together.

» A log for science fair volunteers to record their active and resting heart rates for future experiments.

» A chart of typical resting and active heart rates.

Eating Chocolate for Science

It's easy to forget, but caffeine, a substance added to colas and natural to coffees and chocolate, is actually used in some medical applications as a drug. It is a **stimulant**, so it can stimulate, or speed up, body function. This experiment will test how caffeine affects your resting heart rate.

Do Your Research

This project deals with the effects caffeine has on a person's resting heart rate. Before you begin your project, do some research to find out more about the heart and nervous system, and how the intake of caffeine affects them. Once you've done some research, you can tackle this project. Or, you may come up with your own unique project after you've read and learned more about the topic.

Here are some books and websites you could start with in your research:

» Weinberg, Bennett Alan. *The World of Caffeine.* New York: Routledge, 2002.
» Neuroscience for Kids: Caffeine:
http://www.faculty.washington.edu/chudler/caff.html

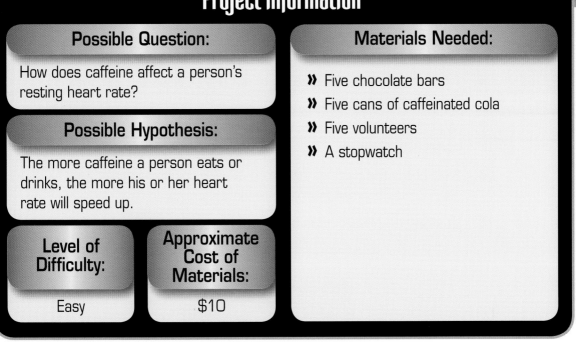

Project Information

Possible Question:

How does caffeine affect a person's resting heart rate?

Possible Hypothesis:

The more caffeine a person eats or drinks, the more his or her heart rate will speed up.

Level of Difficulty:

Easy

Approximate Cost of Materials:

$10

Materials Needed:

» Five chocolate bars
» Five cans of caffeinated cola
» Five volunteers
» A stopwatch

Steps to Success:

1. **NOTE:** Be sure to ask your volunteers if they are diabetic or have any allergies to the foods you'll be using before you begin your experiment. Discuss with your teacher or parents if it is necessary for your volunteers to have permission from their parents.

2. Ask your volunteers to not eat or drink any caffeine for 24 hours before your experiment. You may need to give your volunteers a list of forbidden foods and beverages.

3. Ask your volunteers if they like cola and chocolate and record that information in your research journal.

4. Have your volunteers rest quietly for 15 minutes before you begin. They could read a book or magazine during that time.

5. Take the resting heart rate of each of your volunteers by counting the number of heart beats in 30 seconds. Record the information in your research journal.

Continued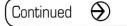

6. Now ask all of your volunteers to eat a chocolate bar and drink a full 8 ounces of cola.

7. Wait 30 minutes, which should be enough time for the effects of caffeine to begin.

8. Now check the resting heart rate of each volunteer again, and record the information in your research journal.

9. Compare the heart rates before and after the effects of caffeine.

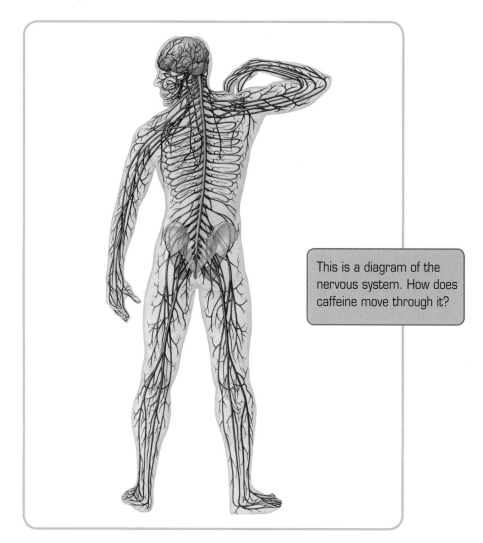

This is a diagram of the nervous system. How does caffeine move through it?

Result Summary:

» Was there a change in your volunteers' resting heart rates after caffeine was consumed?

» Could the change be based on any other variable? Did you notice any nervous energy among your volunteers anticipating the change? Did any of your volunteers have to walk across the room to get the chocolate?

» Did all of your volunteers like chocolate and cola? If not, could that have affected their heart rates?

Added Activities to Give Your Project Extra Punch:

» Do the experiment with double the caffeine and see if the resting heart rates change.

» Do the experiment using caffeine free cola. Do not tell some of the volunteers that there is no caffeine in the cola.

» Wait longer between the time your volunteers eat the caffeine and the time you take their heart rates. Is there a change?

» Try the experiment with half boy and half girl volunteers and see if caffeine has more of an effect on one gender or the other.

Display Extras:

» Heart and nervous system models

» Chocolate bars

» Cola cans

» Other foods with caffeine

» Statistics about caffeine found in your research

Brain Buzz-z-z-z-z

Experts say getting 8 to 10 hours sleep each night helps your brain and body function properly. But what happens if you deny your body the sleep it normally needs? Is your behavior or performance altered by lack of sleep? This experiment will answer some of those questions.

Do Your Research

This project deals with how the amount of sleep a person gets affects the speed and functions of the brain and body. Before you begin your project, do some research to find out more about sleep and what it does for the brain and body. Once you've done some research, you can tackle this project. Or, you may come up with your own unique project after you've read and learned more about the topic.

Here are some books and websites you could start with in your research:

» Esherick, Joan. *Dead on Their Feet: The Health Effects of Sleep Deprivation in Teens.* Broomall, PA: Mason Crest, 2005.
» Stewart, Gail B. *Sleep Disorders.* Farmington Hills, MI: Thompson Gale, 2002.
» Sleep from A to Zzz: http://www.library.thinkquest.org/25553
» Livelyhood: Nightshift: http://www.pbs.org/livelyhood/nightshift

Project Information

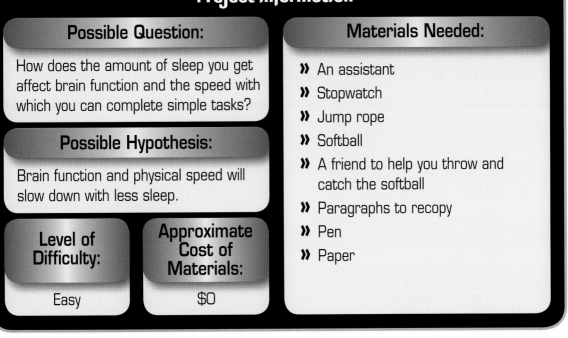

Possible Question:

How does the amount of sleep you get affect brain function and the speed with which you can complete simple tasks?

Possible Hypothesis:

Brain function and physical speed will slow down with less sleep.

Level of Difficulty:

Easy

Approximate Cost of Materials:

$0

Materials Needed:

» An assistant
» Stopwatch
» Jump rope
» Softball
» A friend to help you throw and catch the softball
» Paragraphs to recopy
» Pen
» Paper

Steps to Success:

1. On a day when you are well rested, jump rope for one minute, counting the number of jumps you can complete. Your assistant can handle the stopwatch to keep track of a minute. Record the data.

2. On that same day, have your assistant keep track of a minute on the stopwatch while you see how many times you can catch a softball when your friend tosses it easily from five feet away. Record the data.

3. On that same well-rested day, copy the text of a newspaper article into your research journal for one minute using the stopwatch. Then count how many words you were able to copy and record the data.

4. Again, on the same day, see how many words you can come up with that rhyme with SPOT in one minute. Record the data.

Continued →

5. **NOTE:** Begin the next phase of your experiment on a weekend or other vacation day when you won't fall behind after being deprived of your normal hours of sleep.

6. Go to bed three hours later than you normally go to bed on a school night, but set your alarm clock to wake you at your normal time on a school day.

7. Get out of bed at your normal time for a school day.

8. Repeat the same simple, timed tests you completed in steps 1, 2, 3, and 4.

9. Chart the results on graph paper and in your research journal, both after your normal hours of sleep, and after you deprived yourself of three hours sleep.

10. Repeat the experiment twice, resting a few days in between each experiment, and take an average of the results.

Step 9

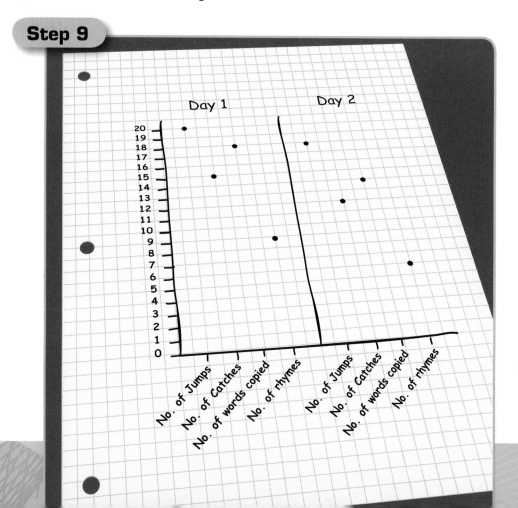

Result Summary:

» Did your scores match? If not, which scores were better?

» Why do you think the results turned out as they did?

» Did the scores change the second and third times you did the experiment? Why or why not?

Added Activities to Give Your Project Extra Punch:

» Record how you felt as you completed the tasks, both on your well-rested day and on your sleep-deprived day and see if there is any difference.

» Repeat the experiment as often as you like, depriving yourself of different amounts of sleep to see how much or how little the differing amounts of sleep will affect your scores.

» Repeat the same tasks on a day when you eat a healthy diet, then on a day when you eat a junk-food diet. Compare the effects of diet and sleep on your scores.

Display Extras:

» The jump rope

» The softball

» The newspaper article

Sneaker Stinker

You may have a favorite basketball player, but would you want to smell his shoes? Nothing clears a room more quickly than someone taking off a pair of sneakers. What causes this stink? This experiment may help solve the mystery of the stinky sneaker.

Do Your Research

This project deals with skin, or the **epidermis**, which is the largest organ of the human body. The project requires you to wrap your foot in a plastic bag, which may affect circulation. If you have any medical conditions, make sure to discuss the project with a parent or doctor before beginning. Before you begin your project, do some research to find out more about skin, its parts, and how they work. Once you've done some research, you can tackle this project. Or, you may come up with your own unique project after you've read and learned more about the topic.

Here are some books and websites you could start with in your research:

» Parker, Steve. *The Senses*. Chicago: Raintree, 2004.

» Rybolt, Thomas R. *Science Fair Success with Scents, Aromas, and Smells*. Berkeley Heights, NJ: Enslow Press, 2002.

» The Sense: http://www.faculty.washington.edu/chudler/chsense.html

» The Sense of Smell: http://www.schoolscience.co.uk/content/5/chemistry/smells/

Project Information

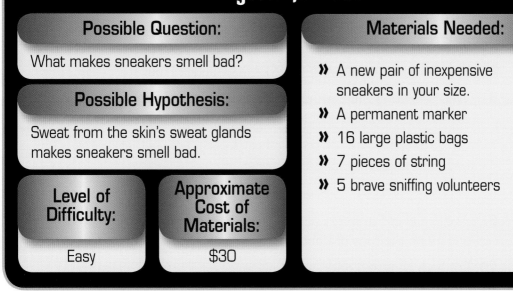

Possible Question:

What makes sneakers smell bad?

Possible Hypothesis:

Sweat from the skin's sweat glands makes sneakers smell bad.

Level of Difficulty:	Approximate Cost of Materials:
Easy	$30

Materials Needed:

» A new pair of inexpensive sneakers in your size.
» A permanent marker
» 16 large plastic bags
» 7 pieces of string
» 5 brave sniffing volunteers

Steps to Success:

1. Buy a new pair of inexpensive sneakers in the right size for your feet.

2. Mark one sneaker with a big X and leave the other without a mark.

3. Before you begin your daily routine, slip the foot matching the sneaker with the X inside two plastic bags, so that your foot is wrapped in a double layer of plastic.

4. Tie a string firmly, but not too tightly, around your ankle to keep the plastic bags from slipping down into your shoe.

Step 3

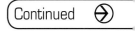
Continued ➔

5. Put the shoe marked with the X on your bagged foot.

6. Wear the other shoe without a sock or any other barrier between your foot and the lining of the shoe.

7. Do 30 jumping jacks or some other physical activity that makes your body, and especially your feet, sweat.

8. Repeat steps 3, 4, 5, 6, and 7 for a full week (7 days).

9. At the end of the week, put each sneaker in a separate plastic bag and tie off the tops of the bags.

10. Put both bags in a dark, moist place for a full week (7 days).

11. At the end of the week, ask your sniffing volunteers to decide which shoe smells worse.

12. Record and graph their reactions as strong, mild, or no reaction in your research journal.

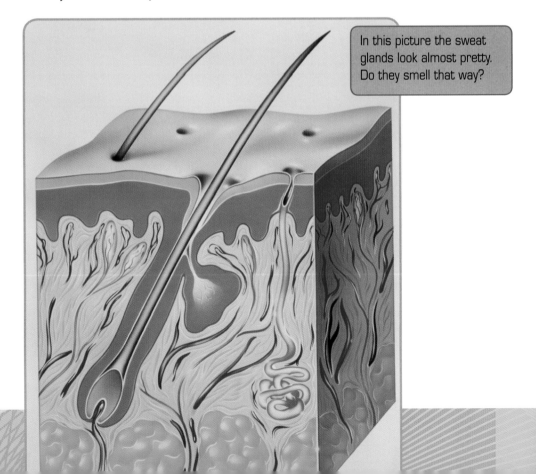

In this picture the sweat glands look almost pretty. Do they smell that way?

Result Summary:

» Which shoe smelled worse at the end of your experiment?

» Did your foot wrapped in plastic sweat more than your other foot?

» Was your plastic-wrapped foot usually hotter or cooler?

» Why did one shoe smell worse than the other?

» Would the results be the same in all people, or would some feet smell worse than others?

Added Activities to Give Your Project Extra Punch:

» Repeat the experiment with a new pair of sneakers, using a sock in one shoe, and no sock in the other. Compare the results.

» Interview a podiatrist (foot doctor) in person or on the Internet about why one shoe smelled different from the other.

Display Extras:

» The experimental sneakers stored in plastic containers to retain the integrity of the smells.

» A model or diagram of the human foot or cross-section of the epidermis.

Don't Look!

Whether it's instinct or learned behavior, one thing is certain. When lights flash, we stop and take notice. But is there an **involuntary** physical reaction to flashing light, or lights of different colors? Is that why storefronts and advertising in big cities use bright lights and neon colors so frequently? This experiment will explore how one part of the body responds — the pupil at the center of the eye.

Do Your Research

This project deals with the human eye and its reaction to light. Before you begin your project, do some research to find out more about the human eye, its parts, and how it works. Once you've done some research, you can tackle this project. Or, you may come up with your own unique project after you've read and learned more about the topic.

Here are some books and websites you could start with in your research:

» Parker, Steve. *The Senses*. Chicago: Raintree, 2004.
» A Big Look at the Eye: http://www.kidshealth.org/kid/body/eye_sw.html
» The Senses: http://www.faculty.washington.edu/chudler/chsense.html

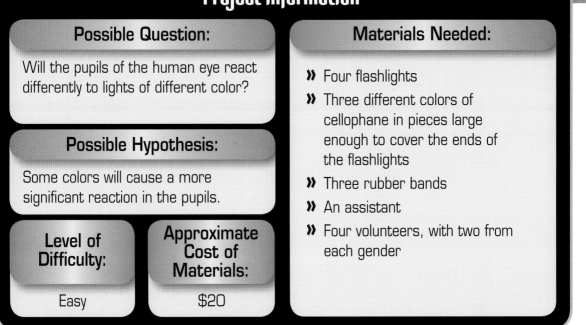

Project Information

Possible Question:

Will the pupils of the human eye react differently to lights of different color?

Possible Hypothesis:

Some colors will cause a more significant reaction in the pupils.

Level of Difficulty:

Easy

Approximate Cost of Materials:

$20

Materials Needed:

» Four flashlights
» Three different colors of cellophane in pieces large enough to cover the ends of the flashlights
» Three rubber bands
» An assistant
» Four volunteers, with two from each gender

Steps to Success:

1. Be sure to fully inform your volunteers in advance of what you plan to do. It will keep them from feeling uneasy as the experiment moves forward.

2. Prepare your pieces of colored cellophane to cover the ends of three of your four flashlights.

3. Wrap the light-end of three of your flashlights each with a different-colored piece of cellophane, using the rubber bands to hold the plastic/cellophane in place to create colored lights.

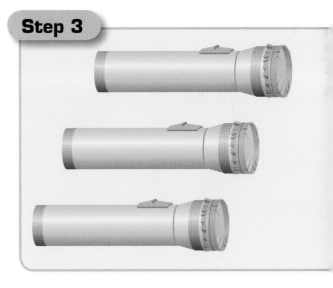

Step 3

Continued →

4. Be sure the room is dimly lit and ask one of your volunteers to come in.

5. Ask him or her to sit down on a chair and relax.

6. Examine and make notes on the look of his or her pupils at this, the start of your experiment. How big is the pupil compared to the iris? How constant is that size as he or she rests? Record the results, including a simple drawing to show the size of the pupils, in your research journal.

7. Tell your volunteer you are going to begin the next phase of the experiment.

8. Have your assistant briefly flash one of the colored flashlights in the direction of the volunteer so he or she can definitely see it. It could be a simple flash of light, or it could be a light turned on for a few seconds and then turned off. Any significant change in the room's lighting will do, but make sure you follow the same procedure each time.

Step 9

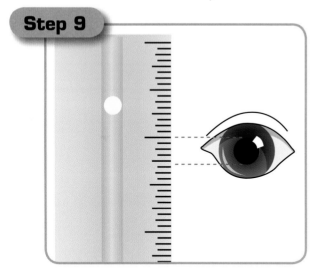

9. Observe your volunteer's reaction, including whether or not his or her pupils change. Record your observations as a drawing or measurement in your research journal.

10. Repeat steps 8 and 9 with each colored flashlight and the regular flashlight, following the exact same procedure each time. Record your observations each time in your research journal.

11. Repeat steps 4 through 10 with each of your remaining volunteers. Again, make sure you are consistent in how you and your assistant use the flashlights with each volunteer.

12. Compare your results.

Result Summary:

» Did different colors of light affect your volunteers' pupils differently?

» Did regular light affect the pupils in the same way?

» Did male and female volunteers have the same reactions?

Added Activities to Give Your Project Extra Punch:

» Repeat the experiment in a brightly lit room, rather than a dimly lit room.

» Add wind to the experiments, using a fan blowing in the volunteer's face, and see if it affects the pupils.

» Test your volunteers using loud sounds instead of light — whistles, the crash of pots and pans, and an air horn could be used. Don't make loud sounds too close to your volunteers' ears though — you wouldn't want to damage their hearing.

Display Extras:

» The flashlights with the plastic wrap/cellophane on them

» A model or diagram of the human eye, with the various parts labeled

» Photos of different pupil sizes based on light reaction

Stop and Catch Your Breath

Our lungs contain almost 1,500 miles of airways and form an important part of breathing. The lungs are the place where our bodies exchange gases between our blood and air. Red blood cells show up and exchange old carbon dioxide your body has made for new oxygen you breathed in from the air. The carbon dioxide goes out with every exhale, and the new oxygen is carried to all the cells in your body. And all this happens without you ever even thinking about it! But, have you ever wondered if all lungs are created equally? This experiment will explore that question.

Do Your Research

This project deals with the lungs, measuring lung capacity, and comparing differences in lung capacity between genders. Before you begin your project, do some research to find out more about the lungs and respiratory system, how they function, and what they do for the human body. Once you've done some research, you can tackle this project. Or, you may come up with your own unique project after you've read and learned more about the topic.

Here are some books and websites you could start with in your research:

» Parker, Steve. *The Lungs and Blood*. Chicago: Raintree, 2004.

» Your Respiratory System: http://yucky.kids.discovery.com/flash/body/pg000138.html

Project Information

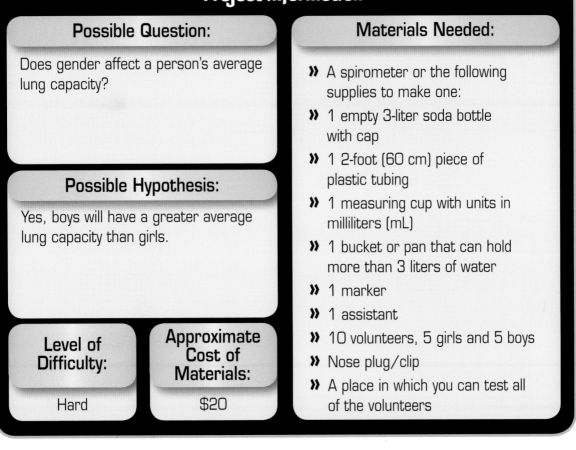

Possible Question:

Does gender affect a person's average lung capacity?

Possible Hypothesis:

Yes, boys will have a greater average lung capacity than girls.

Level of Difficulty:

Hard

Approximate Cost of Materials:

$20

Materials Needed:

» A spirometer or the following supplies to make one:
» 1 empty 3-liter soda bottle with cap
» 1 2-foot (60 cm) piece of plastic tubing
» 1 measuring cup with units in milliliters (mL)
» 1 bucket or pan that can hold more than 3 liters of water
» 1 marker
» 1 assistant
» 10 volunteers, 5 girls and 5 boys
» Nose plug/clip
» A place in which you can test all of the volunteers

Steps to Success:

Make a spirometer:

1. Add half a liter (500 mL) of water to the empty soda bottle using the measuring cup. Draw a line with the marker at the top of the water level. Repeat this two more times, until the bottle is full of water, and then put the cap on. Now you have measuring lines on the bottle.

2. Add enough water to your bucket or pan so that you can submerge the soda bottle.

3. Turn your soda bottle upside down and submerge it in the bucket. Remove the cap under the water. By opening the bottle underwater, you prevent any air from entering the bottle.

Continued ➔

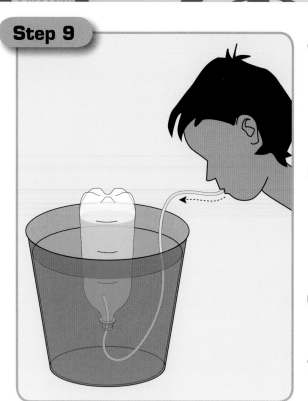

4. Place one end of your plastic tubing into the soda bottle in the water, and leave the other end outside the water. This is the tube your volunteers will breathe into, in order to determine their lung capacity.

5. Make sure you have a place where you can test all ten of your volunteers in one day. You want to make sure that each of your volunteers is breathing the same air, so that your results will be reliable.

6. Tell your volunteers that you'll be testing their lung capacity, one at a time, and recording the results.

7. Have your assistant hold the bottle to keep it from flipping over.

8. Have one of your volunteers put on the nose plug/clip, inhale as much air as he or she can, then exhale this air into the tubing connected to the spirometer.

9. Make a good estimate of the amount of air your volunteer exhaled, remembering that each line on the bottle represents a half liter, starting from the top down.

10. Write this number down in your research journal. This is the amount of air that your volunteer's lungs can hold (lung capacity).

11. Take out the plastic tubing and refill the bottle with water.

12. If it's the same volunteer, reinsert the tubing. **NOTE:** Wash the tubing thoroughly with soap and water before reinserting it between each of your volunteers. Do the same thing with the nose plug/clip. You want to follow good hygiene in your experiment.

Continued ⊕

13. Repeat steps 4 through 9 three times for each volunteer, recording all of the information in your research journal.

14. Calculate an average lung capacity for each of your ten volunteers and record these numbers in your research journal.

15. Calculate an average lung capacity for your boy volunteers, and an average for your girl volunteers. Record that information in your research journal.

Result Summary:

» Based on your data, on average, do boys have a greater lung capacity than girls? Why?

» Did your boy and girl volunteers have similar results in the tests overall, or were there individuals who stood out? Why?

» What might you do differently if you performed the experiment again?

Added Activities to Give Your Project Extra Punch:

» Test volunteers of different ages and see if your results are the same.

» Test athlete volunteers and nonathlete volunteers and see if that makes a difference in average lung capacity.

» Test some volunteers indoors and some outdoors and see if the difference in air leads to different results.

Display Extras:

» The spirometer you made, as well as the nose plug/clip used.

» A model or color diagram of the lungs and respiratory system.

» You probably won't be able to wash everything in between, but if you had disposable mouth pieces to fit on the tubing, you could let people test their lung capacity at your booth during the science fair. You'd simply have to use a new mouthpiece with each person in order to practice good hygiene.

The Competition

Learning is it's own reward, but winning the science fair is pretty fun, too. Here are some things to keep in mind if you want to do well in competition:

1) Creativity counts. Do not simply copy an experiment from this or any other book. You need to change the experiment so that it is uniquely your own.

2) You will need to be able to explain your project to the judges. Being able to talk intelligently about your work will help reassure the judges that you learned something, and did the work yourself. You may have to repeat the same information to different judges, so make sure you have practiced it ahead of time. You will also need to be able to answer the judge's questions about your methods and results.

3) You will need to present your materials in an appealing manner. Discuss with your teacher whether or not it is acceptable to have someone help you with artistic flourishes to your display.

Keep these guidelines in mind for your display:

» **Type and print:** Display the project title, the question, the hypothesis, and the collected data in clean, neatly crafted paper printouts that you can mount on a sturdy poster display.

» **Visibility**: Be sure you print your title and headings in large type and in energetic colors. If your project is about the sun, maybe you'll use bright reds, oranges, and yellows to bring your letters to life. If your project is about plant life, maybe you'll use greens and browns to capture an earthy mood. You want your project to be easily visible in a crowd of other projects.

» **Standing display:** Be sure your display can stand on its own. Office supply stores have thick single-, double-, and triple-section display boards available in several sizes and colors that will work nicely as the canvas for your science fair masterpiece. Mount your core data — your discoveries — on this display, along with photos and other relevant materials (charts, resource articles, interviews, etc.).

» **Dress neatly and comfortably for the fair.** You may be standing on your feet for a long time.

4) The final report is an important part of your project.
Make sure the following things are in your final report:

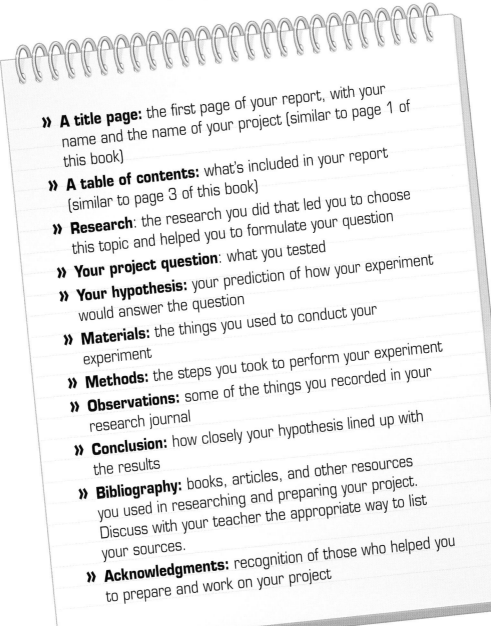

» **A title page:** the first page of your report, with your name and the name of your project (similar to page 1 of this book)

» **A table of contents:** what's included in your report (similar to page 3 of this book)

» **Research**: the research you did that led you to choose this topic and helped you to formulate your question

» **Your project question**: what you tested

» **Your hypothesis:** your prediction of how your experiment would answer the question

» **Materials:** the things you used to conduct your experiment

» **Methods:** the steps you took to perform your experiment

» **Observations:** some of the things you recorded in your research journal

» **Conclusion:** how closely your hypothesis lined up with the results

» **Bibliography:** books, articles, and other resources you used in researching and preparing your project. Discuss with your teacher the appropriate way to list your sources.

» **Acknowledgments:** recognition of those who helped you to prepare and work on your project

Prepare to Be Judged

Each science fair is different but you will probably be assigned points based on the categories below. Make sure to talk to your teacher about how your specific science fair will be judged. Ask yourself the questions in each category to see if you've done the best possible job.

Your objectives

» Did you present original, creative ideas?

» Did you state the problem or question clearly?

» Did you define the variables and use controls?

» Did you relate your research to the problem or question?

Your skills

» Do you understand your results?

» Did you do your own work? It's OK for an adult to help you for safety reasons, but not to do the work for you. If you cannot explain the experiment, the equipment, and the steps you took, the judges may not believe you did your own work.

Data collection and interpretation

» Did you keep a research journal?

» Was your experiment planned correctly to collect what you needed?

» Did you correctly interpret your results?

» Could someone else repeat the experiment?

» Are your conclusions based only on the results of your experiment?

Presentation

» Is your display attractive and complete?

» Do you have a complete report?

» Did you use reliable sources and document them correctly?

» Can you answer questions about your work?